DRAG!
Friction and Resistance

Stephanie Paris

Consultants

Timothy Rasinski, Ph.D.
Kent State University

Lori Oczkus
Literacy Consultant

Katie McKissick
Physical Science Consultant

Based on writing from
TIME For Kids. TIME For Kids and the *TIME For Kids* logo are registered trademarks of TIME Inc. Used under license.

Publishing Credits

Dona Herweck Rice, *Editor-in-Chief*
Lee Aucoin, *Creative Director*
Jamey Acosta, *Senior Editor*
Heidi Fiedler, *Editor*
Lexa Hoang, *Designer*
Stephanie Reid, *Photo Editor*
Emily Engle, *Contributing Author*
Rachelle Cracchiolo, *M.S.Ed., Publisher*

Image Credits: pp.11 (top, bottom), 15 (top), 30, 34, 42, 52–53, 55 (all) Alamy; pp.10, 35 (right), 57 (bottom), 44–45 iStockphoto; p.53 (top & middle) Toru Yamanaka/AFP/Getty Images/Newscom; pp.44, 47 NASA; pp.9, 13, 22–23, 28–29, 36–37, 38–39 (bottom), 48–49 (illustrations) Timothy J. Bradley; pp.48–49 (top) Andrejs Pidjass/NejroN/Getty Images/iStockphoto; p.50 Paul Lampard/Getty Images/ iStockphoto; p.52 (bottom) Gary Hincks/ Photo Researchers, Inc.; All other images from Shutterstock.

Teacher Created Materials

5301 Oceanus Drive
Huntington Beach, CA 92649-1030
http://www.tcmpub.com

ISBN 978-1-4333-4940-9

© 2013 Teacher Created Materials, Inc.

Table of Contents

A World Without Friction!

Imagine sitting on a couch at home. You decide to stand up, but when you try to push off the ground, your feet slip out from under you. Everything is as slippery as ice. Luckily, the couch is wedged against a wall, so you push hard and manage to bounce onto the floor. But now you have another problem because you are sliding toward the door and you can't stop! You slip out the door, down the stairs, and down the street.

THINK LINK

✦ What is friction?

✦ Where do you encounter friction?

✦ How can we increase or decrease friction?

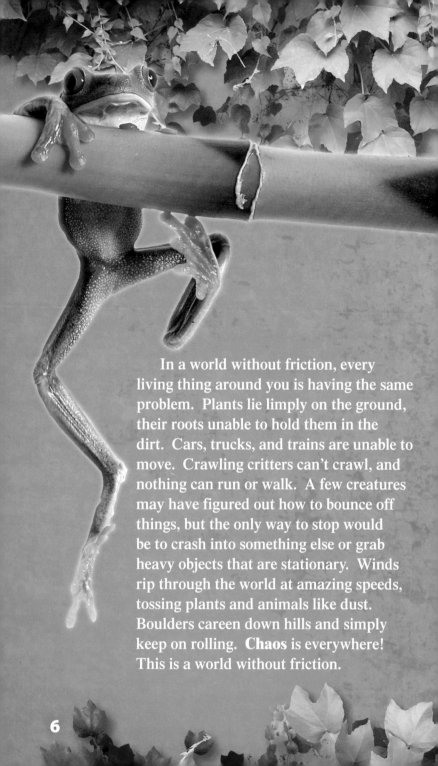

In a world without friction, every living thing around you is having the same problem. Plants lie limply on the ground, their roots unable to hold them in the dirt. Cars, trucks, and trains are unable to move. Crawling critters can't crawl, and nothing can run or walk. A few creatures may have figured out how to bounce off things, but the only way to stop would be to crash into something else or grab heavy objects that are stationary. Winds rip through the world at amazing speeds, tossing plants and animals like dust. Boulders careen down hills and simply keep on rolling. **Chaos** is everywhere! This is a world without friction.

Could Life Survive?

A world without friction would be very different from the one we know. Many people wonder if life would even be possible. Could animals breathe without friction? Could cells interact? Would blood pump? How would living things get the food and nutrients they need? As you read about friction, think about how it affects life on Earth.

> " A gem cannot be polished without friction, nor a man perfected without trials. "
> —Lucius Annaeus Seneca, philosopher

Types of Friction

No matter where you are or what you are doing, there are **forces** at work all around you, all the time. *Force* means "active power." In physics, friction is often thought of as a negative force. Friction is the result of two objects rubbing up against each other. It happens because two surfaces in close contact grip each other. This gripping occurs all the way down at the **molecular** level, but it happens at larger levels, too. Because of this gripping, friction can slow things down and make them stop moving.

If tires don't properly grip the road, a car can slide and a driver can lose control.

Push and Pull

Most forces can be thought of as either a push or a pull. The force of gravity pulls an object toward Earth. You push off the ground to get yourself moving.

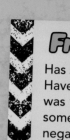

Friction Gets a Bad Rap!

Has something ever "rubbed you the wrong way"? Have you ever entered a room and known there was "friction between two people" there? People sometimes use the idea of friction to describe negative feelings.

When sandpaper and wood are rubbed together, it creates a lot of friction.

WOOD

SANDPAPER

When wood is rubbed against a smoother substance such as glass, there is less friction.

WOOD

GLASS

Static Friction

Have you ever used a felt board? Felt objects are arranged on a flat surface, such as a piece of cardboard, that is also covered with felt. If you position the board upright, the objects remain where they are placed. A felt board relies on **static friction** to function properly. Static friction is the force of friction that exists when two objects are not moving. Try putting a flat eraser on your book. If you tilt the book up slightly, the eraser won't move. This is static friction at work. Static friction is the strongest kind of friction.

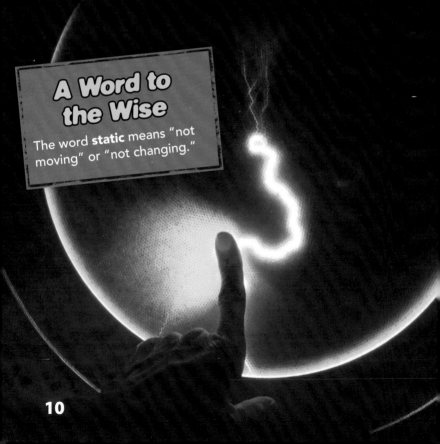

A Word to the Wise

The word **static** means "not moving" or "not changing."

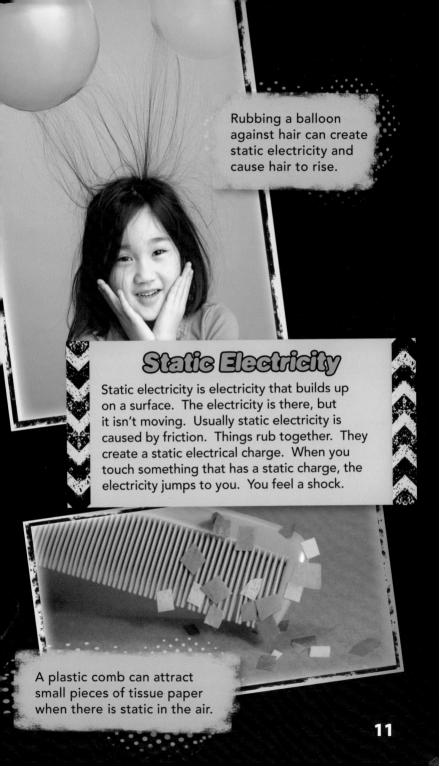

Rubbing a balloon against hair can create static electricity and cause hair to rise.

Static Electricity

Static electricity is electricity that builds up on a surface. The electricity is there, but it isn't moving. Usually static electricity is caused by friction. Things rub together. They create a static electrical charge. When you touch something that has a static charge, the electricity jumps to you. You feel a shock.

A plastic comb can attract small pieces of tissue paper when there is static in the air.

Sliding Friction

Sliding friction happens when two objects slide past each other. Think of pushing a brick across the ground or a book across your desk. The force that prevents these things from moving along smoothly is sliding friction. Sliding friction is a strong force. It can take a lot of energy to keep something moving when it is working against sliding friction.

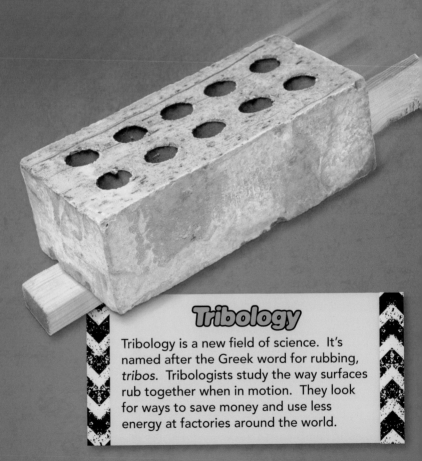

Tribology

Tribology is a new field of science. It's named after the Greek word for rubbing, *tribos*. Tribologists study the way surfaces rub together when in motion. They look for ways to save money and use less energy at factories around the world.

Fold a sheet of paper into a small rectangle and place it on a book. Tilt the book up slightly, and the paper doesn't move. Static friction holds it in place.

Keep tilting your book up, and soon the paper will start to slide. At that moment, sliding friction is at work. How steeply must you tilt the book to make the paper slide?

Now, try doing the same exercise with a paper clip. Does it start sliding at the same angle? What about an eraser? Do you think the results would be the same with a different type of book?

Rolling Friction

Rolling friction is the force that works against motion when one object rolls along another object. Without rolling friction, we couldn't control a soccer ball or travel from place to place in a car. The ball or the car would just keep moving on and on. Rolling friction works to slow things down, just like sliding friction, but it is a weaker force. That means if all conditions are the same, it takes less force to keep a rolling object moving than a sliding one.

Ancient Wheels

So far, the oldest wheel ever found was discovered in the area that once was Mesopotamia. It is thought to be over 5,000 years old!

Inventing the Wheel

Ancient builders discovered if they placed a fallen tree trunk under something and rolled it, they could move it more easily. They also learned to use a **sledge**, which was made from wood and used to drag heavy things. People combined the sledge with the rolling logs by dragging the sledge over the logs. Then, someone thought of making an axle and attaching the two parts. The first cart was born! And sliding friction was exchanged for rolling friction.

Fluid Friction

Everything is made of molecules. In solids, these molecules are close together and don't move very much, but in gases and liquids, these molecules are farther apart and move a lot. They tend to flow, which is why gases and liquids are called **fluids**. Fluid means "flowing."

Water and air are both fluids. When something such as a boat moves through a fluid, some of the molecules simply move around it without any problem, but many of the molecules also bash into it. They bounce into each other and build up, creating pressure. They pull on the surface, slowing it down and resisting movement. For this reason, fluid friction is often described as **air resistance** or **water resistance**.

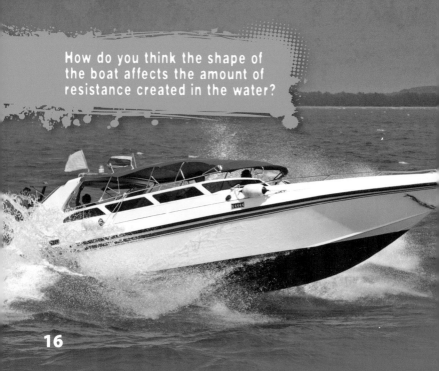

How do you think the shape of the boat affects the amount of resistance created in the water?

Viscosity of Common Fluids (cP)

Low Viscosity ↑

0.3	acetone (nail polish remover)
1	water
10	blood
10,000	chocolate syrup
50,000	ketchup
250,000	peanut butter

High Viscosity ↓

Viscosity is a measure of a fluid's resistance to flow. Something that flows quickly has a low viscosity. Something that flows slowly has a high viscosity. Viscosity can be described in relation to water and measured in centipoise (cP). Water has a viscosity of 1 cP.

Hall of Friction Fame

Spiders, worms, and geckos are just some of the animals that use friction to survive. Whether they use it underground or high on the ceiling, friction makes these creepy crawlies a force to be reckoned with.

Spider

Have you ever wondered just how the itsy bitsy spider climbed up the water spout? The answer is that a spider has extremely small hairs on its feet. These hairs grip onto a surface and build sliding friction. They keep the spider from sliding down the surface.

Earthworm

An earthworm uses the moisture in soil to create **mucus**. This mucus covers the earthworm's body. It helps reduce the friction between the earthworm and the soil it lives in. With reduced friction, the earthworm can travel easily in the soil.

Gecko

A gecko has millions of hair-like organs on its toes. Just like a spider, these tiny organs create a lot of friction between a gecko's feet and a surface. As a result, a gecko can run across ceilings. It can even hold on to a vertical wall with just one toe!

What Affects Friction?

Is friction always the same? Of course not! Several factors affect the amount of friction that results when two objects come in contact with one another.

Imagine rubbing two smooth pieces of metal together. Now think about rubbing two rough bricks together. Which items do you think will create more friction? The **texture** of objects has a lot to do with how much friction they make. Moving objects across a rough surface creates more friction. Moving things over a smooth surface produces less friction.

Try This

Locate two wooden blocks and attach sandpaper to one side of the blocks. Now, try rubbing the plain wood sides together. Feel how much force it takes to make them slip past each other.

Next, turn the blocks over to the sandpapered side. Try rubbing the rough sides against each other. Again, feel the force between the two blocks.

Is it easier to rub the smooth wood or the rougher sandpaper?

Icy Showdown

Did you know that ice arenas are kept at different temperatures, based on who is going to be using them? The temperature affects the friction between the skates and the ice!

When hockey teams are on the ice, arenas keep the ice extra cold so the ice is smoother and harder. This makes it easier to control the puck.

When figure skaters are on the ice, the ice is kept a little warmer. This makes the ice softer, rougher, and easier to land on after big jumps.

Roll It

In this experiment, you will roll a model car down a ramp coated with different surfaces.

Materials

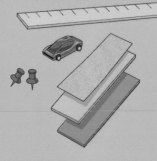

- a small toy car with wheels that move freely
- pushpins
- three strips of different-texture surfaces (plastic, sandpaper, carpet, felt, or wood)
- a flat board
- a block or stack of books
- a yardstick

Step 1

Prop the board up on a block or stack of books to create a ramp with a small incline. Place the car at the top of the ramp and let it go. (Don't push it.)

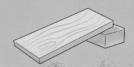

Step 2

Using the yardstick, measure the distance the car traveled past the edge of the ramp. Record your results. Repeat two more times.

- Which surface was the slowest? Which was the fastest? How does that relate to how far the car traveled?

- Which surface had the most friction? Which had the least?

- What could you do to reduce friction in this test?

Step 3

Without changing the angle of the board, attach one of the surfaces to the ramp. Again, place the car at the top, and without pushing, allow it to roll. Measure the distance the car went. Record your results in a chart similar to the one below. Repeat this procedure with each of the other surfaces.

Results

Surface	Distance Trial 1	Distance Trial 2	Distance Trial 3
Bare Board			
Surface 1			
Surface 2			
Surface 3			

Pressure

Friction increases with pressure. For example, if bicycle brakes are touching the wheels of a bike lightly, nothing much will happen. But if you squeeze the brake handles, the brake pads will press on the wheels. With the increased pressure, the wheels will slow and quickly stop.

> " No pressure, no diamonds.
> —Thomas Carlyle, writer "

Tough Treasures

The diamonds found in mines were formed over one billion years ago. Extreme heat and pressure deep below Earth's surface turned carbon into crystals. Underground volcanoes pushed the diamonds toward the surface. Today, scientists can make these super-strong stones in a lab!

Weight

Weight is the force of gravity exerted on something based on its mass. On Earth, you can consider this to be how much an object presses down toward Earth. In other words, weight is a kind of pressure. Since increasing pressure increases friction, increasing weight does the same thing.

Shopping Carts

Have you ever pushed a shopping cart at the market? At first, when the cart is empty, you can easily zip around. But after the cart is filled with heavy items, it becomes much harder to push. The wheels may even drag on the floor instead of rolling easily. There is more friction when the cart is full and heavy than when it is empty and light.

Try This

Try using the sandpaper blocks again. This time, rub the sandpapered sides of the blocks together using different amounts of pressure. Start off lightly. Then, press harder. How does the friction change? Now, try the wooden side of the blocks. Again, start with light pressure, and then press harder. Is there a noticeable difference? Why?

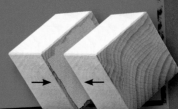

Lubrication

Because of friction, all machines break at some point. Pieces rub together, and parts wear down. But any car owner will tell you one of the best things you can do to keep a machine running well is to make sure it is well lubricated. **Lubricants** reduce friction by making things slippery. A lubricant can be something as simple as water. Think of sliding down a waterslide. You slip down the slide because water is acting as a lubricant, but water is thin and **evaporates** quickly. Engines use special oils that stick to the parts and won't evaporate or burn in the heat. Grease, oil, and silicone are all common lubricants.

turbo engine

An Engine Without Oil?

What happens to a car engine when it is run without oil? The moving parts rub together so much that at first, little tiny pieces start to rub off and clog the engine. The engine gets very hot very quickly. Parts start to melt and get weaker. Soon, parts get worn down and break apart, sending pieces of metal flying into other parts. In a matter of seconds, the engine has ripped itself apart from the inside!

Slick as a Pencil

One of the best lubricants for extremely high or extremely low heat is made from graphite. That's the same stuff in your pencil.

Good to the Last Drop

Have you ever tried to get the last bit of ketchup out of a bottle? Usually, you have to shake and pound the container. And even then, you probably won't get it all. Friction holds it in. But researchers have created a new food-safe coating that solves this problem. The super-slippery stuff lets ketchup—or any gel or liquid—slip easily out of the bottle right down to the last drop.

How Lubricants Work

Machines are all around us. Parts whir and move past each other, sometimes at very high speeds! Friction is always between them, stealing their energy and breaking them down. Lubricants help machines fight friction. But how do they work?

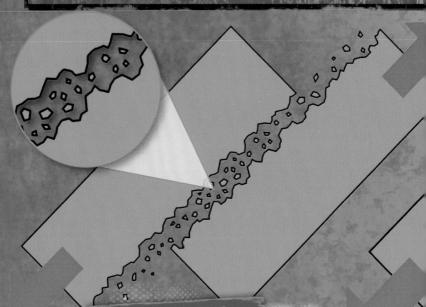

Solids Rub Together

Solids may look smooth on the surface, but seen under the microscope, they are full of little pits and ridges that catch on each other. Since solids don't change shape, the only way they can transform is by heating up and breaking.

Fluids Can Flow

A fluid such as grease or water can flow between the layers of the solid. This makes a cushion that helps smooth out the little bits and pieces that might rub together.

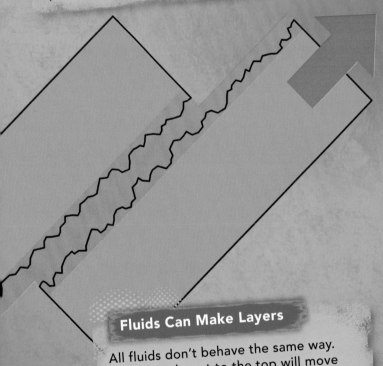

Fluids Can Make Layers

All fluids don't behave the same way. The layer closest to the top will move with the top piece of the machine. The layer at the bottom will move with the bottom piece. This lets them slide past each other easily without catching on the middle layer, which is also a fluid.

Area of Contact

Think about a quilted blanket. When the blanket is open, the surface area is large. Each place that touches the bed presses down lightly because the weight is spread out. If you fold up the quilt, it has a smaller surface area. It doesn't touch as much of the ground, but it presses down more in each place it touches since the weight is more concentrated. Think about the quilt at a molecular level. When the quilt is folded, the same number of molecules are pushing against the bed as if the quilt were spread flat.

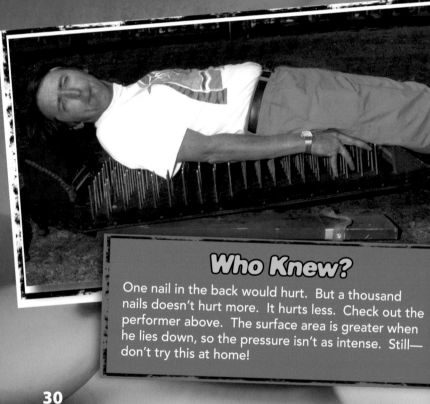

Who Knew?

One nail in the back would hurt. But a thousand nails doesn't hurt more. It hurts less. Check out the performer above. The surface area is greater when he lies down, so the pressure isn't as intense. Still—don't try this at home!

Ball Bearings

Surface area doesn't change friction. But the amount of contact between two objects at the molecular level does. Ball bearings are rings of hard metal balls inside a metal track. In a ball bearing, the amount of contact between the balls and the moving parts is very small, so the friction is very low. This lets things move more easily. Machines, roller skates, and even cars use ball bearings to keep friction low.

In Motion

All cars use friction to stop. And the many variables that affect friction can be seen during this important action. Just like the brakes on a bike, auto brake pads press on the wheels to slow and stop the vehicle. How far the car travels once the brakes are applied is called the **braking distance**. The speed and weight of the car as well as whether the road is wet or dry can affect the braking distance.

brake

Stopping Distance

Brakes don't start working until someone presses the brake pedal. People need time to notice a hazard. Then, they must think about stopping. Finally, it takes a moment for the message to get from the brain to the foot so the driver can step on the brake pedal. Together, this process makes up the driver's **reaction time**. The **stopping distance** for a car is a combination of the driver's reaction time and the braking distance for the vehicle.

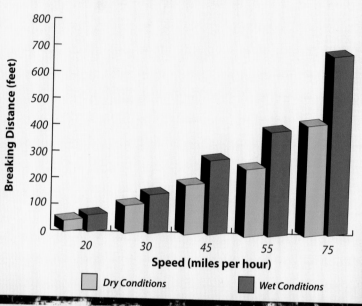

Dry Versus Wet

This chart compares actual braking distances on a particular stretch of pavement during dry and wet conditions. Which conditions appear to create more friction?

Breaking Distance (feet) (y-axis: 0, 100, 200, 300, 400, 500, 600, 700, 800)

Speed (miles per hour) (x-axis: 20, 30, 45, 55, 75)

Dry Conditions · Wet Conditions

What a Drag!

Have you ever put your hand out the window as you rode in a car? The rush of air that pulls your hand to the back of the window is called **drag**. Compare the force you feel when your hand is parallel to the ground. You can also try holding your hand straight up to see how drag increases when the position of your hand changes.

Drag is another word for air and water resistance. When you pull a box over a rough patch of ground, the box and the ground grip each other the same amount of force no matter how fast you pull. In contrast, if you are pushing through a fluid, the fluid resists, but it also moves out of the way. If you go slowly, the molecules are given more time to adjust, so they push back less. If you move quickly through air or water, the molecules build up quickly and don't move smoothly. They can't get out of the way, so they swirl around and create greater drag.

At the Racetrack

Have you ever seen a race car that was moving so fast it needed a parachute to help it stop? Race cars are designed to reduce drag as much as possible. Drivers want to go down the track quickly using little fuel. But this means that when it is time to stop, traditional brakes may not do the job. Luckily, parachutes work very efficiently at high speeds. They slow the car before it reaches the end of the track.

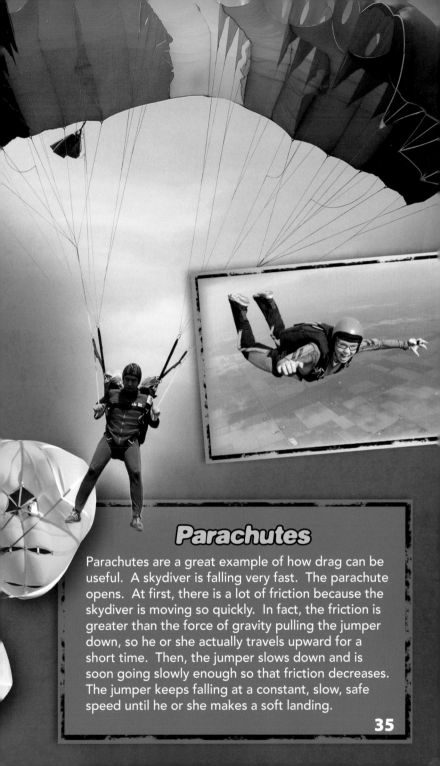

Parachutes

Parachutes are a great example of how drag can be useful. A skydiver is falling very fast. The parachute opens. At first, there is a lot of friction because the skydiver is moving so quickly. In fact, the friction is greater than the force of gravity pulling the jumper down, so he or she actually travels upward for a short time. Then, the jumper slows down and is soon going slowly enough so that friction decreases. The jumper keeps falling at a constant, slow, safe speed until he or she makes a soft landing.

35

Drafting: The Science of Speed

NASCAR drivers understand a lot about friction and drag. They make a living by driving fast. Forces that decrease their speed (such as drag caused by friction) must be avoided! One way they do this is by **drafting**.

Eyes on the Prize

Drafting helps two cars go faster. But no NASCAR driver wants another driver to win. They will help someone go faster by drafting because they also benefit. After the two cars get in front of the pack, each driver will make a move to finish first!

What?

Drafting is when one car drives closely behind another car—not simply a few feet away but a few inches away.

Why?

When a driver drafts another car, he or she is decreasing the drag on both cars. It is as if the air is passing over just one car rather than two. The result is that both engines work together to move both cars more quickly down the track.

Where?

NASCAR drivers can draft on any track, but it is most common at the Daytona and Talladega speedways. These are long tracks with steep banks, which means the racers could be in danger of driving too fast. Drivers are forced to decrease the horsepower of their cars on these tracks. Drivers are frustrated that the lower horsepower limits their speed. So they draft to make up for it!

The Difference a Shape Makes

Have you ever noticed that rockets, airplanes, and submarines all have a long, **tapered** shape? This shape moves through fluids well. There are not many places for molecules to get caught, so the **streamlined** shape reduces drag.

Blowing in the Wind

This graphic shows how a fluid flows around different shapes. When the fluid must move around lots of corners and curves, it pulls on the object and creates more resistance. But the more smoothly the fluid flows around the shape, the less resistance there is.

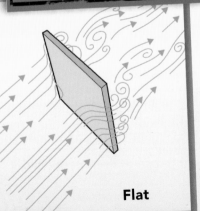

Flat

Round

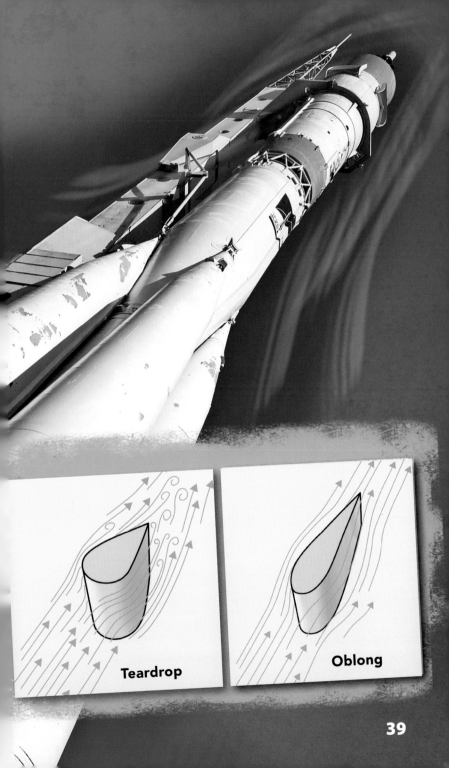

Teardrop

Oblong

Streamlining Survival

Machines aren't the only things that take advantage of streamlining. Animals do, too. Of course, these animals haven't copied machines. The engineers designing submarines and rockets looked to these animals to see what shapes work best.

dolphins

stingray

penguins

Birds have streamlined bodies, hollow bones, and flat wings that help them soar and glide through the sky.

hawk

falcon

sea lion

bluefin tuna

Streamlined bodies move faster. That makes it easier for these animals to capture prey and escape predators. They also use less energy getting around.

What Does Friction Do?

Friction resists motion and slows things down. So, what else does it do? One thing friction does is create heat. When two objects rub together, all the **kinetic energy** gets transformed into heat instead. This can be useful if you're trying to build a fire, but it can also mean a lot of energy is wasted in the form of heat.

$E = mc^2$

$E = mc^2$ is Albert Einstein's very famous formula. It says that energy (E) is equal to mass (m) times the speed of light (c) squared. This means that matter can be turned into energy and energy can be turned into matter. Not only that, but matter has a lot of energy in it. Unfortunately, we aren't very good at using all that energy. Most of it escapes unused. And one of the most common ways it escapes is through heat.

Try This

It's easy to generate heat with friction. Just rub your hands together! It doesn't take very long to notice the heat building up as the molecules pull against each other. Now, try rubbing your hands on different surfaces. Try rubbing them on your pants and the desktop. Do they heat up at different rates?

What If?

Car designers spend a lot time figuring out how to keep engines cool. After a long trip, the engine and even the tires are too hot to touch safely. But what if all that energy could be used? What if it could be turned into movement instead? Cars could be very efficient indeed.

Lifesaver

Clearly, friction is very important. After all, it allows us to stop objects in motion, but it is equally important because it lets us move. Once again, think of standing and walking without the friction necessary to allow your feet to make contact with the ground. You could push off solid objects, but there would be no way to control your direction or stop. Car tires wouldn't work because they couldn't roll. Inside our bodies, cells rely on friction for many of their functions as well. It might be possible for life to exist on a planet without friction, but it would not look like the life we know!

Slipping into Space

Whenever two objects come in contact, there is friction involved. But out in space, there are vast distances between things. There isn't even air out there! So it is possible to move in space without experiencing friction at all.

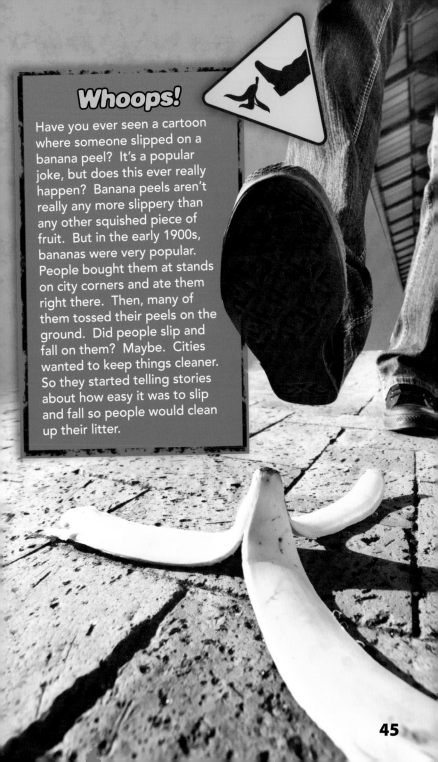

Whoops!

Have you ever seen a cartoon where someone slipped on a banana peel? It's a popular joke, but does this ever really happen? Banana peels aren't really any more slippery than any other squished piece of fruit. But in the early 1900s, bananas were very popular. People bought them at stands on city corners and ate them right there. Then, many of them tossed their peels on the ground. Did people slip and fall on them? Maybe. Cities wanted to keep things cleaner. So they started telling stories about how easy it was to slip and fall so people would clean up their litter.

45

Friction and Meteors

Friction also helps life on Earth survive the impact of thousands of **meteors** each year. When a meteor enters Earth's atmosphere, it is going so fast that the impact is very violent. The meteor experiences strong friction from the gases around Earth. It starts to burn up and becomes a giant fireball. Most meteors burn up and never make it to the surface of Earth. Those that do are called meteorites. They are a fraction of their original size. Mostly, they land safely in the ocean. You can see what would happen in a location that does not have the friction of the atmosphere to protect it by studying the moon. The moon's craters are places where space rocks crashed into the surface.

Discovering Hoba

The largest meteorite on Earth was found in 1920 by a farmer plowing his field. His plow ran right into the 60-ton iron meteorite! Scientists excavated the meteorite to study it, but it has never been moved from the spot where it was discovered. It is much too big. The meteorite is named Hoba after the name of the farm where it sits.

Feel the Burn

When a space shuttle reenters the atmosphere, it goes through the same intense friction as a meteor. So why doesn't a space shuttle burn up like a meteor? Part of the reason is because it is made of special materials that can withstand high temperatures. But it is also because of the shape of the shuttle. The **blunt** surface faces down and actually creates a shock wave that keeps the heat away from the shuttle.

Weather

The air moving high above Earth is not affected much by the surface of the planet. It moves smoothly and quickly, but when wind closer to Earth flows around lakes, oceans, mountains, houses, and trees, resistance occurs. The air swirls in many directions and becomes **turbulent**. The thin layer of atmosphere closest to Earth is called the **friction layer**.

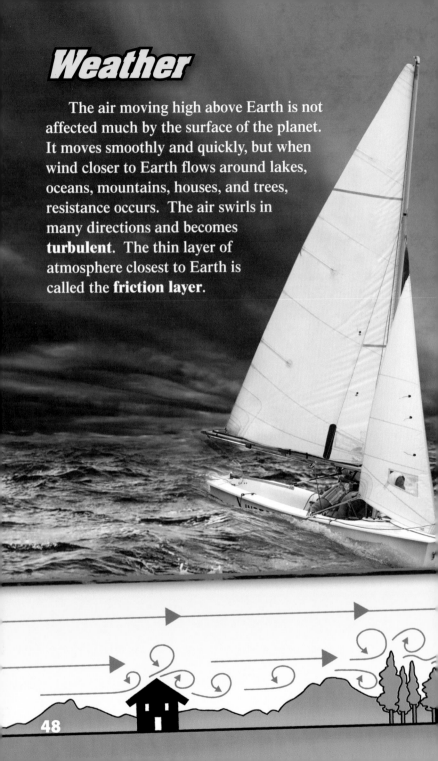

Wind Basics

Wind is caused when warm, light air rises and cooler, heavier air sinks. As they pass each other, the different pockets of air make a sort of loop. But it isn't that simple. Earth is rotating. Different parts are getting warmer and cooler all the time. Also, moist air acts differently from how dry air does. Predicting weather can be very complicated!

Air flows in different patterns depending on what is in its path.

Shocking Effects

Have you ever dragged your feet along a carpet and then touched a doorknob? Did you get an electric shock? The friction from dragging your feet can cause an electrical charge to build up on your body. When you touch another object, the charge is released as a tiny spark, jumping from your finger to the object.

Scientists still argue over exactly how lightning is formed, but most think it is basically this same process. The air and water particles in a storm rub together and create an electrical charge. But this is no tiny spark. When it gets released, the electricity is a huge lightning bolt!

Counting the Miles

You can tell how far away a flash of lightning is by counting the seconds from the time you see it until you hear the sound of thunder. Wait for a lightning flash. Then, count one-one-thousand, two-one-thousand, three-one-thousand until you hear the thunder. Every five seconds is equal to one mile between you and the storm.

Thunder Rolls

When lightning forms, it heats the air around it and creates pressure rapidly. This starts a sound wave that takes the form of thunder. Sound waves take longer to travel than light. So unless the lightning is striking very close to you, you will hear the thunder several seconds or more after you see the lightning.

Shake, Rattle, and Roll!

Friction can cause a tiny spark or a huge earthquake. An earthquake happens when two of Earth's plates slide past each other. Friction causes the jagged edges of Earth's plates to stick together. The force of friction makes them resist movement. But while the jagged edges are stuck together, they are storing up energy. Eventually, the energy grows so strong that it overcomes the force of friction. The plates move. All the energy that was stored up is released in waves and causes the Earth to move. We experience the movement as an earthquake.

When Earth's plates shift, friction can build up in dramatic ways.

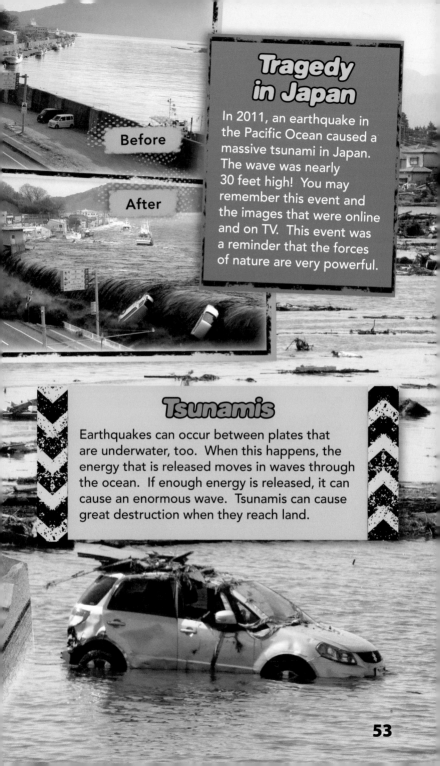

Tragedy in Japan

In 2011, an earthquake in the Pacific Ocean caused a massive tsunami in Japan. The wave was nearly 30 feet high! You may remember this event and the images that were online and on TV. This event was a reminder that the forces of nature are very powerful.

Before

After

Tsunamis

Earthquakes can occur between plates that are underwater, too. When this happens, the energy that is released moves in waves through the ocean. If enough energy is released, it can cause an enormous wave. Tsunamis can cause great destruction when they reach land.

Sounds of Friction

Friction isn't simply destructive. It also makes life beautiful—through music! Did you know that many instruments rely on friction to make their sounds?

Bowed Stringed Instruments

The bow rubs against the strings, causing vibrations that make sound.

Washboard

Musicians rub their fingernails over the washboard.

Musical Saw

The bow rubs against the smooth edge of the saw blade while the musician bends the saw to alter the pitch.

Tuned Wineglasses

Musicians rub damp fingers round the rim of glasses filled with different amounts of water, causing vibrations from the friction.

Friction Drums

Players use a cork or stick to create friction on the head of the drum.

Don't Hold Back!

Remember, the same force that allows us to stop also helps us move. And the same force that breaks down the machines we rely on also allows life to exist. Forces are power. And every force can be a powerful tool for the person who understands how it works and how it can be used.

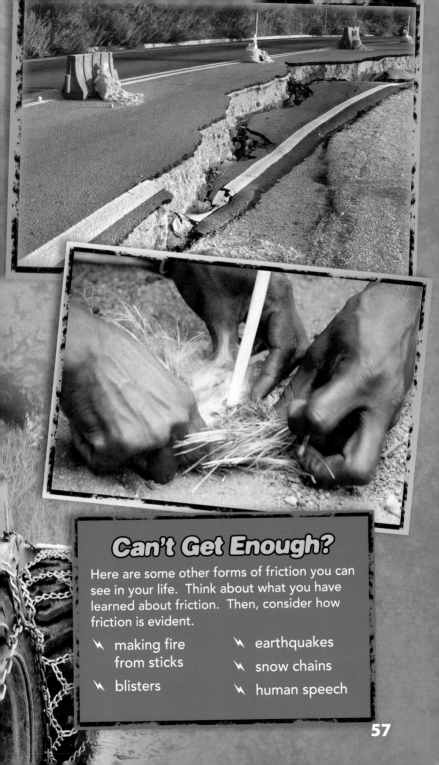

Can't Get Enough?

Here are some other forms of friction you can see in your life. Think about what you have learned about friction. Then, consider how friction is evident.

- making fire from sticks
- blisters
- earthquakes
- snow chains
- human speech

Glossary

air resistance—the friction between air molecules and things moving through them

blunt—having a dull edge or end; not sharp

braking distance—the distance a vehicle travels after the brakes have been engaged

chaos—complete confusion and randomness

drafting—using the pocket of reduced air pressure behind a moving object to increase speed

drag—the force that acts against the movement of an object

evaporates—changes from liquid to vapor or gas

fluids—matter that has the ability to flow or be poured

forces—active powers that cause motion or change

friction layer—the layer of atmosphere closest to Earth

kinetic energy—the energy of movement

lubricants—substances such as oil or grease that reduce friction

meteors—pieces of rock or metal from outer space that burn as they enter Earth's atmosphere

molecular—relating to the smallest possible part of a substance

mucus—a slippery sticky substance produced to moisten and protect the body

reaction time—the amount of time it takes for a person to notice a hazard, think, and send a message to the body to react

rolling friction—the kind of friction that resists motion between objects that are rolling against each other

sledge—a basic vehicle with runners to help move heavy things over dirt or snow; a sled

sliding friction—the kind of friction that resists motion between objects that are sliding past each other

static—not moving or changing

static friction—the strongest kind of friction; the friction between two things that are not moving

stopping distance—braking distance plus reaction time

streamlined—shaped to allow fluids or air to flow around smoothly

texture—the structure, feel, and appearance of something

tapered—gradually getting smaller at one end

turbulent—unsettled; not calm

viscosity—a measure of a fluid's resistance to flow

water resistance—the friction between water molecules and things moving through them

weight—the force of gravity exerted on something based on its mass or the matter in it

Index

Bibliography

Graham, John. *Forces and Motion (Hands-on Science).* **Kingfisher, 2001.**

Explore the physics of gravity, friction, centrifugal force, and more. You'll learn about simple machines and complex inventions through the 40 hands-on experiments in this book.

Greathouse, Lisa. *How Toys Work: Forces and Motion (Science Readers).* **Teacher Created Materials, 2009.**

This book explores electric, magnetic, and motion-powered toys from design to function. It introduces readers to six simple machines and explains how they use force and motion to do work. Learn about time-honored favorites including the rocking horse, Slinky, and rattles.

Leslie-Pelecky, Diandra. *The Physics of NASCAR: The Science Behind the Speed.* **Plume, 2009.**

NASCAR is more than just an exciting sport you watch on TV. There is a lot of science that goes into keeping the drivers safe and making the cars move fast.

Oxlade, Chris. *Friction and Resistance (Fantastic Forces).* **Heinemann-Raintree, 2006.**

Do you know how parachutes work? This book asks the questions about friction that you want answered. Don't forget to test out the experiments, too!

More to Explore

How Lizards Defy Gravity

http://www.pitara.com/discover/eureka/online.asp?story=97

Geckos are interesting little creatures. Find out more about this little lizard that can hang upside down with ease.

How Water Slides Work

http://science.howstuffworks.com/engineering/structural/water-slide.htm

Water slides rely on physics, gravity, and friction to function. Take away just one of those elements and you won't have the same fun. Learn how these three things work together to give you a wild and fun ride.

The Science of Earthquakes

http://earthquake.usgs.gov/learn/kids/eqscience.php

A large-scale example of friction happens during an earthquake. The science behind an earthquake is explained in detail at this site, with diagrams and images to help you visualize the concepts.

Sid the Science Kid: Fun With Friction

http://pbskids.org/sid/funwithfriction.html

Help Gerald knock over household items using force and friction. You choose the floor surface, and he'll slide the block. Try to choose the surface with the right amount of friction.

About the Author

Stephanie Paris is a seventh-generation Californian. She has her BA in psychology from the University of California, Santa Cruz, and her multiple-subject teaching credential from San Jose State University. She has been an elementary classroom teacher, an elementary school computer and technology teacher, a home-schooling mother, an educational activist, an educational author, a web designer, a blogger, and a Girl Scout leader. Ms. Paris lives in Germany, where the word for *friction* is *friktion*.